T0054077

What Was Hurricane Katrina?

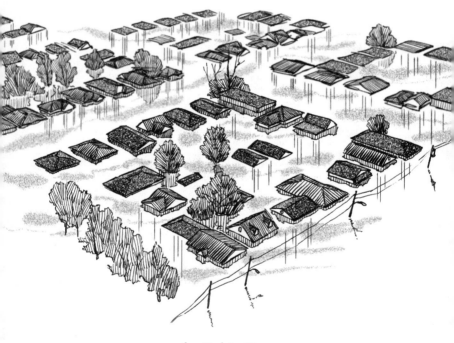

by Robin Koontz

illustrated by John Hinderliter

Penguin Workshop
An Imprint of Penguin Random House

To my Alabama kin, and the memory of our
precious times at the shore—RK

For Rose, who hates scary stuff—JH

PENGUIN WORKSHOP
An imprint of Penguin Random House LLC, New York

First published in the United States of America by Penguin Workshop,
an imprint of Penguin Random House LLC, New York, 2015

Text copyright © 2015, 2018, 2021 by Robin Koontz
Illustrations copyright © 2015, 2018 by Penguin Random House LLC

Visit us online at penguinrandomhouse.com.

Library of Congress Control Number: 2015015988

Printed in the United States of America

ISBN 9780448486628   15 14 13 12 11 10

Contents

What Was Hurricane Katrina?

Monday, August 29, 2005

It was very early Monday morning in New Orleans, Louisiana. Rain had been pounding all night. The wind was blowing harder and harder. The day before, the mayor of the city had sent a warning to all the people in New Orleans. Everyone had to get out. A monster storm was on its way!

All weekend, cars had crowded the streets. Gas stations had lines of people waiting to fill up. Highways became jammed with one-way traffic going north, out of New Orleans. Those who stayed behind crouched in their attics, if they had one. Others waited in shelters, hotels, and hospitals. Many thousands were crowded together, either in a huge stadium or the city convention center. Almost everyone had known for several days that a bad storm was on its way. But no one realized how bad. Katrina was more

than a savage hurricane. It was a superstorm. By late Monday afternoon, most of New Orleans was flooded, and the water still kept rising.

Water poured into homes and rose higher as people cut their way to the rooftops. Entire neighborhoods were flooded and destroyed. Tens of thousands were stranded, many without food or water. Roads and bridges were gone. There was no power. Telephone lines failed. Most cell phones stopped working. People couldn't turn on a TV or a radio to find out what was going on.

People waited for help on rooftops and in trees, and sometimes help never came. Others were trapped inside their houses. People drowned in the streets of their own neighborhoods. Over a million people became homeless, and over eight hundred thousand homes were destroyed. Hurricane Katrina turned out to be the most destructive storm in the history of the United States. It was also one of the most deadly—the best guess is that 1,900 people lost their lives because of the storm. Sadly, many of those lives could have been saved.

Early-Warning System

National Hurricane Center

Storms like Katrina can be tracked and measured by satellite, radar, aircraft, and other means. The National Hurricane Center studies the behavior and paths of every storm it spots. Its main job is to provide an early-warning system. Then the public can prepare for what might be coming its way. Meteorologists, scientists who study weather, use a scale to measure hurricanes. The scale is based mostly on the storm's wind speed. There are five categories of hurricanes. Category 1 is the weakest. Category 5 is the most powerful, with winds at more than 155 miles per hour. Katrina was a Category 5.

CHAPTER 1
Just a Little Storm

Hurricane Katrina began on August 19 as a tropical disturbance. That means it was just a little storm with winds blowing in every direction.

Meteorologists watched the little storm move across the Atlantic Ocean from the west coast of Africa, north of the equator. They knew that hurricanes form in warm, moist air. Ocean water north of the equator during late summer is perfect for hurricanes.

By the time the little storm got close to the Bahamas late on August 22, 2005, it was stronger. Winds whipped at about twenty-five miles per hour, making small trees sway.

About two days later, the storm moved northwest through the Bahamas with winds of about forty miles per hour. A wind that strong is hard to walk in. Trees can lose small branches. The storm also rotated in a circle. It was at this point that the tropical storm was named Katrina. And it was heading toward South Florida.

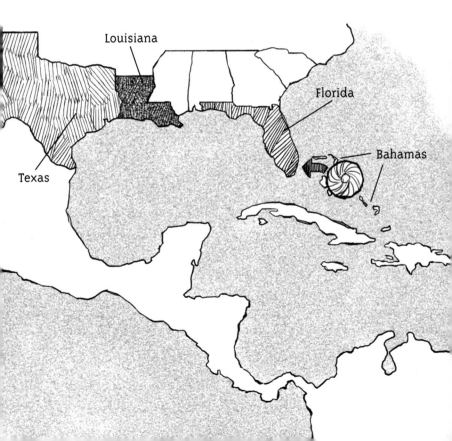

Hurricane Names

Hurricanes have been given names since 1953. It is an easy way to report their progress. Before hurricanes had names, it got confusing when more than one storm was being tracked. Six lists of 21 different names are used. The names are in alphabetical order and switch between male and female names. If all the names on a list are used up in one season, the next storms are named for letters in the Greek alphabet. Names of the most severe storms, like Katrina, are retired.

Retired Hurricane Names as of 2018

Agnes	Cesar	Fabian	Hattie	Ivan	Mitch
Alicia	Charley	Felix	Hazel	Janet	Nate
Allen	Cleo	Fifi	Hilda	Jeanne	Noel
Allison	Connie	Flora	Hortense	Joan	Opal
Andrew	David	Floyd	Hugo	Joaquin	Otto
Anita	Dean	Fran	Igor	Juan	Paloma
Audrey	Dennis	Frances	Ike	Katrina	Rita
Betsy	Diana	Frederic	Inez	Klaus	Roxanne
Beulah	Diane	Georges	Ingrid	Lenny	Sandy
Bob	Donna	Gilbert	Ione	Lili	Stan
Camille	Dora	Gloria	Irene	Luis	Tomas
Carla	Edna	Gracie	Irma	Maria	Wilma
Carmen	Elena	Greta	Iris	Marilyn	
Carol	Eloise	Gustav	Isabel	Matthew	
Celia	Erika	Harvey	Isidore	Michelle	

Florida

By August 25, Katrina was close to becoming a hurricane. Hurricanes have powerful winds of at least seventy-four miles per hour. (They are called *cyclones* in some areas of the world and *typhoons* in others.) Their fierce winds rotate around a center core called the *eye*. Winds that strong can uproot trees, toss cars around, and blow the roofs off houses!

Hurricanes form in the North Atlantic Ocean in late spring, summer, and early fall. They occur most often between mid-August and October.

These unwelcome visitors can blow into land areas in the Caribbean Sea, the Gulf of Mexico, and the North Atlantic.

Most storms weaken when they reach land. That's because they no longer are getting power from warm ocean air. Katrina, however, got stronger as it blew its way to southern Florida on August 25. The powerful storm turned into a hurricane about two hours before it landed, causing flooding and several deaths. Even so, at that point, Katrina was still not considered an unusual storm.

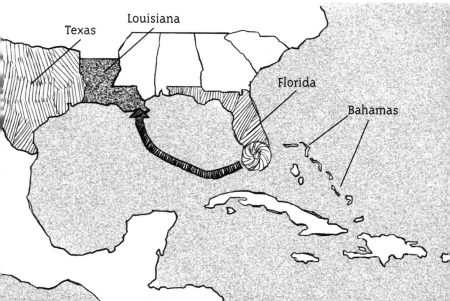

Unfortunately, Katrina was just getting started. As the storm traveled farther west over the Gulf of Mexico, it wound through an area called the Loop Current, gaining more strength from deep warm water. It grew wider, covering a larger and larger area. And the winds rotated faster and faster.

Max Mayfield was the National Hurricane Center director. He was very worried. It wasn't just the damage from high winds and rain that concerned him. When a hurricane reaches land, it will push a wall of ocean water along with it. This wall of water is called a *storm surge*.

Mayfield saw that Katrina was moving straight toward New Orleans, the largest city in Louisiana.

Max
Mayfield

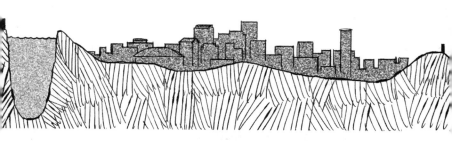

A huge storm surge there would spell disaster. Why?

New Orleans is shaped like a huge soup bowl and is nearly surrounded by water. Much of the city lies at or below sea level. If water gets in, terrible flooding can occur.

To keep water out, the city was protected by barriers called *levees*. But even before Hurricane Katrina hit, there was doubt about whether the levees would stand up to a superstorm. Parts of the levee system had been recently rebuilt. The new structures had not yet been tested by a hurricane as powerful as Katrina. Water could be pumped out if the storm surge went over the levees. But what if the levees broke or collapsed? That would mean terrible trouble.

Levees

Levees are structures people build along a waterway to keep floodwaters from entering dry land. They can be constructed from natural soil or artificial materials such as concrete or steel. Flood walls, usually made of concrete or steel, are often built to add to the height of a levee. A levee system can include other structures, such as floodgates and canals, which help reduce the risk of flooding.

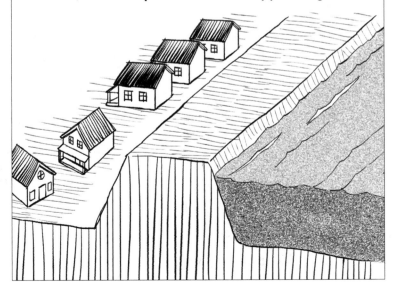

Ray Nagin

On Saturday evening, August 27, Max Mayfield called Ray Nagin, the mayor of New Orleans, Kathleen Blanco, the governor of Louisiana, and the governor of Mississippi, Haley Barbour. He urged them to tell people to get out of the area: A monster storm was coming! But Mayor Nagin did not want to order people to leave. He worried about what would happen if hotels and businesses were left empty. He worried about crime. So instead, he urged people to leave, but did not order them to do so. The choice was up to them.

At 10:11 a.m. on Sunday, August 28, the National Weather Service issued the most serious warning yet to people who were in Southeastern Louisiana and the Mississippi Gulf Coast: "URGENT WEATHER MESSAGE . . . HURRICANE KATRINA . . . A MOST POWERFUL HURRICANE WITH UNPRECEDENTED STRENGTH . . ." (*Unprecedented* means "never before seen.")

The message warned what would happen. Wood-frame buildings would be completely destroyed, and concrete structures would be severely damaged. Windows would blow out, and houses could explode. The air would be filled with flying debris, including trees, refrigerators, and even cars! Anyone outside faced almost certain death.

Katrina had become a Category 5 hurricane. Now the hurricane had winds of 175 miles per hour! That's as fast as a high-speed train. At this point, Mayor Nagin ordered the first mandatory evacuation in New Orleans's history. *Mandatory* means that leaving the city was no longer a choice. *Evacuation* means getting out. The mayor told the city residents, "We're facing the storm most of us have feared."

CHAPTER 2
New Orleans

New Orleans is located in a small area between the Mississippi River, the Gulf of Mexico, and Lake Pontchartrain. Lake Pontchartrain connects to the Gulf of Mexico.

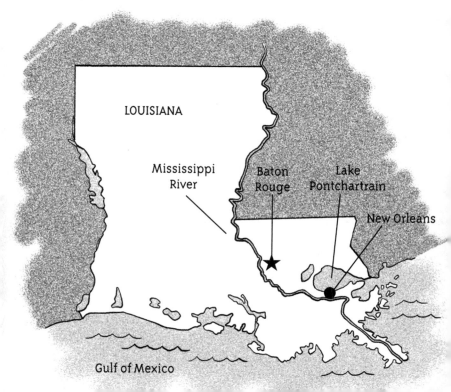

LOUISIANA

Mississippi River

Baton Rouge

Lake Pontchartrain

New Orleans

Gulf of Mexico

Native Americans first settled the area. They lived on a delta that was formed by the Mississippi River. *Deltas* are triangle-shaped landforms created from soil deposits from surrounding water. This delta's location was a perfect place for a city to grow! The locals traded with people who traveled between the Mississippi River and Lake Pontchartrain.

France claimed the area in the 1680s. The city of New Orleans was soon formed and became the capital of French Louisiana. When the Spanish acquired the territory in 1763, they designed buildings that used native brick-and-tile roofs, some of which can still be seen today.

New Orleans has always been home to many different peoples. Besides Native Americans and the French and Spanish, people from Caribbean islands such as Haiti arrived. So did slaves from West Africa, some of whom were able to buy freedom in New Orleans.

After Thomas Jefferson bought Louisiana from France in 1803, the area became part of the United States. Yet the different cultures in New Orleans remained strong. Because of this, New Orleans is one of the most interesting cities in the United States. Its diverse history is celebrated,

Thomas Jefferson

and it's responsible for the area's great music, spicy cooking, dialects (ways of speaking), and religious festivals. "Let the good times roll" is the motto of the city, which is also called the Big Easy.

Jackson Square

New Orleans is a great city, but also a city with a lot of poverty. It is divided up into neighborhoods called wards. There are seventeen wards altogether, some located on high ground and others on low ground.

The richest neighborhoods, such as the Garden District, are on higher ground, while the poorer neighborhoods are on low ground.

Garden District

In 2004, more than two-thirds of the population of New Orleans was black. Middle-class African Americans tended to live in the eastern half of the city. The poorest African Americans lived mostly near swampy marshlands or—like people in the Ninth Ward—along the riverfront. Parts of the

Lower Ninth Ward actually lay about four feet below sea level. In a superstorm, that meant the Lower Ninth would get flooded. Over the years, there was flooding from many hurricanes in New Orleans. But when Hurricane Betsy slammed the gulf in 1965 and sent floodwaters smashing through levees all around the city, it was a wake-up call. It became evident that more needed to be done to protect New Orleans.

Lower Ninth Ward

Government money helped pay for a better levee system. The Army Corps of Engineers set out to build a levee system that would withstand a serious flood. Stronger, taller levees were built, and old systems were repaired or improved. The goal was to help protect New Orleans from another storm like Hurricane Betsy.

Unfortunately, new problems arose. The new levees and dams held back dirt from the wetlands. *Wetlands* are places where water covers the soil. This made it easier for water to surge into the city during a big storm. And Katrina promised to be the biggest of the big.

CHAPTER 3
Too Little, Too Late

After the order from the mayor, about 1.2 million people from the New Orleans area left. Thousands more had already gone, days before the storm was due to land. They left their homes and possessions behind. They fled the city in their cars. Others escaped using city buses, some

of it provided by the government. By Saturday, highways were set up for one-way traffic: out. Rows of cars and buses were bumper-to-bumper in all the highway lanes. It was a slow process. A lot of people had come to visit for the Labor Day holiday week. Now vehicles streamed out of the city all day and all night. About 80 percent of the 484,000 people living in the center of the city managed to get out.

Earlier, there were mandatory evacuation orders in the low-lying coastal parishes in metropolitan New Orleans and surrounding areas. There were also orders from local governments in Alabama and Mississippi telling everyone living in low-lying areas to move to higher ground and into shelters. Thanks to the orders in those areas, there were fewer people left behind to face Hurricane Katrina.

Unfortunately, 100,000 people remained behind, even after the order to leave.

Why didn't everyone in New Orleans get out?
There were lots of reasons. Many had not heard
the terrible news. The early winds and rain had
knocked out power. So many residents had no
TV, radio, or telephone to warn them of danger.

Some chose to stay, despite the order to leave.
They had survived other storms and thought they
could do so again. Others wanted to protect their
property. In the past, they had left only to return
to homes that were damaged and burglarized.

Some people didn't want to leave their pets behind. Others stayed because they had to care for loved ones who could not be moved safely. For thousands and thousands of others, however, there was no choice. They had to stay because they had no way to leave.

When Katrina hit, about a quarter of the people of New Orleans lived in poverty. They had no car or no money to fill their car up with gas. Being prepared for a superstorm meant stocking up on supplies like food and medicine. However, many didn't have the money to do that.

A lot of people lived on fixed incomes, and their monthly funds were already spent by the time the hurricane arrived. As

for public transportation, by Sunday, buses and trains had been canceled. The airport had been closed as the hurricane winds got closer. Hattie Johns, a New Orleans resident, told a news reporter, "I know they're saying 'get out of town,' but I don't have any way to get out."

People with special needs—the elderly in wheelchairs, for instance—found themselves in even greater danger. The city decided to move them to local shelters to wait out the storm. Often, their caregivers stayed by their side.

By Sunday evening, Katrina loomed ever closer to the city as it whipped north through the Gulf of Mexico. The Federal Emergency Management Agency (FEMA) had sent supplies to shelters and other locations in the Gulf Coast states in advance of the storm. Supplies included truckloads of water, ice, and meals ready to eat, called *MREs*. Several other emergency response agencies set up medical teams with supplies and equipment.

Unfortunately, all that was done was not nearly enough.

By Sunday afternoon, it was too late to leave the city. The Louisiana Superdome—where football games were played—was turned into a shelter. But it was called a "shelter of last resort." That meant people should go there only if they had no other safe place. At first the Superdome was intended just for people with special needs, but thousands of people showed up. There were over ten thousand people in the dome by late Sunday evening.

Katrina was due to strike the city early on Monday morning.

FEMA

The Federal Emergency Management Agency (FEMA) was formed in 1979. It combined earlier disaster relief agencies. Its job is to deal with natural disasters such as a hurricanes or earthquakes, as well as man-made disasters, such as the terrorist attacks on September 11, 2001. FEMA helps local and state agencies with disasters in their areas. It contributes funds for rebuilding. FEMA also provides low-interest loans so people can rebuild a destroyed home or buy a new one. But in the days, weeks, and months after Hurricane Katrina, FEMA was widely criticized for its slow response to the storm. In 2006, the US Congress passed the Post-Katrina Emergency Management Reform Act. It created leadership positions and position requirements, set out new laws, and enhanced FEMA's responsibility.

CHAPTER 4
The Storm Hits!

At about 6:00 a.m. on Monday, Katrina made landfall in southeast Louisiana. *Landfall* is where the center of the hurricane crosses the coastline. Katrina was down to a Category 3 storm now, but still a killer. The storm kept traveling farther west at about fifteen miles per hour.

Over a hundred miles wide, it uprooted trees and tore apart buildings and houses. Windows shattered and some houses exploded from the storm pressure. Heavy rains continued to pound the streets. In New Orleans, boats from the storm surge crested over the levees and slammed into buildings. Roads and bridges were damaged or destroyed. Many buildings were left with only their steel skeleton remaining.

The winds and rain knocked out electricity. Streets everywhere were filled with fallen trees and power lines. In New Orleans, a water main was broken because of the hurricane. That meant there was no safe drinking water.

The Louisiana Superdome was also damaged by the storm. The high-speed winds peeled away a large part of the roof. Rain poured in on the many thousands of people inside.

The gulf water that Katrina passed over before hitting land was shallow. Shallow water causes very powerful storm surges. Storms that come in from deeper seas do not push as much water onto land.

As Katrina moved over land on Monday morning, the water it brought along surged into the gulf and into Lake Pontchartrain. Several feet of water spilled over levees and into communities along the northeastern shore of New Orleans. A storm surge of up to nineteen feet hit two neighborhoods. People climbed to the roofs of their houses to escape the storm surges. They waited to be rescued, often watching all their possessions float away.

Katrina became weaker as it moved inland in the early afternoon. But it still caused a lot of rain and thunderstorms. Flood watches and warnings were issued from the Gulf Coast to the Ohio Valley. Now called Tropical Storm Katrina, it also produced over thirty tornadoes. The tornadoes caused a huge amount of damage in the state of Georgia and other areas.

Tornadoes versus Hurricanes

Tornadoes are vertical columns of very fast-moving air. A tornado spins violently. Generally, it can be seen only if it picks up dust and debris, which it often does. Thunderstorms and hurricanes can create tornadoes from air that rises into the storm clouds. The winds closer to land slow down more quickly than the winds that are spinning higher up. This causes vertical pressure that can become a tornado.

Although narrow, tornadoes are the most violent of all storms. They can spin 200 to 300 miles per hour. That's twice as fast as a Category 5 hurricane!

Which is worse? Hurricanes might not be as violent, but they cover more ground. And they stick around longer, causing more damage over a wider area. A tornado usually lasts only about ten minutes, though there are more of them, too. About 1,000 tornadoes and an average of about seventeen hurricanes strike the United States each year.

Hurricane Katrina was not the most powerful hurricane to strike the Gulf Coast. But it was the most destructive in US history. It caused damage throughout Louisiana and Mississippi, into Florida, Alabama, and Georgia. Coastal towns like Biloxi and Gulfport, both in Mississippi, were nearly destroyed. Little was left other than piles of wood and rubble where buildings once stood. Remains of boats, cars, and even parade floats littered the streets.

By late Monday afternoon, the worst seemed to be over. The storm was down to a Category 1. Unfortunately, that didn't spell relief for New Orleans.

In fact, the most terrible day for the city and its residents was still to come.

CHAPTER 5
The Levees

People in New Orleans knew that water from storm surges could spill over the levees. And with Katrina, it did. This is called *overtopping*. But they also knew that in the past, water had been pumped out quickly. Pumping stations and drainage canals were all over the city. The pumping stations took away water from rainfall and storm surges. The water left the city through canals.

But what was supposed to work didn't this time. The pressure from the surges against the weaker parts of the levee system was too great.

Even before the biggest surge broke through at 8:30 a.m. on Monday, some levees breached. *Breaching* is when parts of the structures break away. The levees in the Lower Ninth Ward breached in several places. The explosive sounds caused some survivors to think that the levees were being blown up!

Tons of water from the breaches blasted into the low-lying neighborhoods. Houses became completely submerged in water. Hundreds of people drowned within hours. Thousands of others scrambled to grab floating debris, fighting for their lives in the torrent of water. Why did the levees fail?

Many of the 350 miles of levees around New Orleans had been built with silt. Silt is made mostly of fine sand—it's simply not strong enough to hold up against a tremendous surge.

Plus, many levees were built on top of marshland. The marshlands didn't provide a strong enough foundation. Water was able to seep through cracks and under the weak foundation.

Some levee systems held up better than others. The ones along the Mississippi River survived most of the storm surges. But the ones that were supposed to protect the city from Lake Pontchartrain and the gulf were not as successful. Water seeped in underneath them.

Many other levee systems were old and needed repair. In some places, there were nothing but sandbags. Sometimes a new levee was attached to an old levee, like a patchwork quilt. A lot of the failures in the levees happened where old and new met.

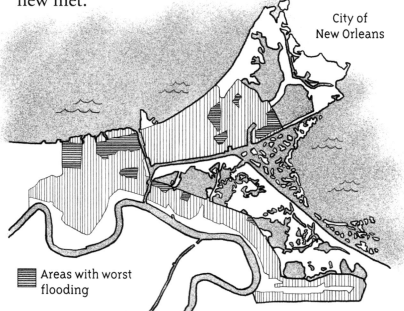

City of New Orleans

Areas with worst flooding

The map to the left shows which areas of the city were hit hardest with flooding. (They are shown with dark shading.) On the morning of August 29, the water level in New Orleans was rising, not falling. Even without getting any news, the people in the Ninth Ward knew exactly what was happening. They could see it. Water was pouring into their neighborhood, long after the storm had passed.

In addition to the breaching, most of the pumping stations were flooded. Power to run them was gone. And in some places, the people who were in charge of the pumping stations were also gone. So water kept coming in, but no water was going out.

In a few hours, the floodwater in many areas of New Orleans was so deep that the second stories of houses were underwater. People had to chop through ceilings in order to escape through their roofs. Anyone who went to bed Monday night thinking the worst was over was wrong.

On Tuesday, August 30, the water was still rising.

By Wednesday, August 31, more than 80 percent of New Orleans was flooded. The water finally stopped rising once it reached the same level as Lake Pontchartrain. The historical areas were high and dry. But most of the neighborhoods built in the twentieth century were submerged. As bad as the storm was, the failure of the levees became an even bigger news story than Katrina!

CHAPTER 6
Stranded

More than one hundred thousand people in New Orleans needed help. Flood survivors faced new dangers. They could still drown in their homes or in the streets. They might starve or get sick from the heat. They might die from lack of freshwater or medical attention. So far, they had lost everything but their lives. For many, it would be days before help arrived.

For the most part, the first rescue efforts were carried out by local agencies. City and state workers usually got to flooded areas the quickest. The US Coast Guard was involved, too, sending helicopters to rescue people from rooftops. They were also busy taking emergency supplies to shelters throughout the Gulf Coast.

Hundreds of volunteers chipped in to help neighbors. Unfortunately, the New Orleans Fire Department had no boats. And the police department owned just five. So local people used their own boats or found abandoned ones and rowed around rescuing people. Some were able to offer food and water. People with medical skills helped those who needed attention.

Federal agencies, such as the Department of Homeland Security and FEMA, were slow to recognize just how bad things were in New

Orleans. President Bush was visiting Texas and other places when Hurricane Katrina hit and the levees failed. He was later criticized for not returning earlier to handle the disaster. He finally flew over the flooded city on his way back on Wednesday, August 31. Finally, real rescue efforts got under way.

Meanwhile, the Superdome was overflowing, and more people were still coming in. By Wednesday, August 31, as many as twenty-three thousand people were housed there. Nobody really knows just how many were there, because some were moved to other shelters while others were still being picked up from the flooded streets and simply dropped off on higher ground with no supplies or shelter.

The "refuge of last resort" was not meant to provide shelter for several days. But that's what happened, because people had no other place to go. There was not enough food or water to take care of all the people. Plumbing backed up, and toilets failed to work. The only power was from emergency generators. There was no air-conditioning. The temperature outdoors was in the high eighties. Indoors, the heat was almost unbearable.

Life Inside the Superdome

The Superdome is a multilevel building. Thousands of people camped on the bottom level. Others made spaces on the seats and on the upper levels. The huge building was messy, smelly, hot, and dark. But people did the best they could.

Adults were given two bottles of water a day. Everyone lined up for boxed meals. National Guard soldiers handed them out. Sometimes there wasn't enough food to go around.

Garbage and human waste was everywhere. Some say that fights broke out. But most who were there said that people got along. They helped each other. Some cared for the ones who could not care for themselves. And everyone kept wondering the same thing: How long would they be stuck there?

Finally, officials at the Superdome started turning away people because they feared there was no room left. Beginning on Monday, when the flooding started, thousands also headed for the Ernest N. Morial Convention Center. It was located on high ground. However, it was not an official refuge. There was no food or water other than what people brought with them.

There were no emergency teams or law enforcement. As many as nineteen thousand people were staying in the convention center. Yet somehow, not until Thursday, September 1, did FEMA Director Michael Brown claim to know about survivors housed there.

Days went by. Thousands of people camped in rescue shelters or just lived on the streets above the floodwaters. Later, people said that they felt like they had been abandoned. Their lives had been spared, and they were grateful for that. But the government was not doing enough to help them.

The lack of law enforcement and the angry mood sparked fights and crime. People looted stores, taking water, food, clothing, and camping supplies. Some people took advantage of the situation and stole other items, but most stole for survival.

Governor Kathleen Blanco of Louisiana was trying to rescue her citizens. She was in touch

Kathleen Blanco

with FEMA. Five hundred buses were promised, but none arrived before Wednesday evening. She let local officials take any buses they could find to help people get out of the flooded city. She also allowed people to move into hotel rooms and cruise ships. Many people were taken out of the city to safer shelters. Finally, on Thursday morning, the FEMA buses arrived. Slowly, the rescue efforts continued.

With water in the city standing three feet above sea level, thousands of homes were six to nine feet deep in a murky brew of water, mud, and garbage. Until the levees could be patched and the water pumped out, much of New Orleans would remain underwater.

Underwater Neighborhood

A neighborhood called St. Bernard Parish is located in southeast New Orleans. Katrina left it entirely underwater! There had been more than twenty-six thousand homes. Approximately eight remained in livable condition. The water that had flooded the parish was dirty. There had been a large oil spill from a storage tank. Even when the water was finally pumped out, the parish was covered in slick, oily mud.

CHAPTER 7
The Blame Game

Once the storm called Katrina was gone, a new storm started. It was a blaming storm. Who was to blame for what had happened? There were plenty of suspects.

It became clear that an early forced evacuation would have saved many lives. The state and city governments should have helped many more people leave much sooner. Then emergency responders would have been able to focus on the hardest-hit areas.

It took too long for the federal government to help New Orleans. Late Monday, Mayor Nagin sent a long list of emergency aid requests to FEMA. But the supplies and assistance did not arrive for days, if ever. Governor Blanco sent the White House a long list of needed supplies and personnel. Officials didn't respond to the governor's requests for help until the next day.

This was a national emergency, yet President George W. Bush was not informed of the failed levees until around midnight on Monday.

In the days following Hurricane Katrina, there was a lack of communication, conflicts over who should be in charge, and mass confusion among the local, state, and federal agencies. While officials argued over what to do and who should do it, thousands of people suffered, trapped inside the flooded city. It was an overall failure of all the agencies to have a common goal and a plan, both before and after the hurricane.

The French Quarter of New Orleans

Jazz musicians celebrate Mardi Gras in the French Quarter

Satellite image of Hurricane Katrina over Louisiana

Storm damage on the Gulf Coast

A home destroyed by Katrina

A bridge is destroyed by storm winds

A single chair sits among the wreckage

The roof of a home is torn off

Crews work to repair a break in one of the levees

An Air Force helicopter flies over a flooded neighborhood

A man flees to the roof of his car to escape rising floodwaters

ROAD DETOUR

Flooded roads in New Orleans

New Orleans residents make their way to the Superdome

Storm survivors write messages to rescue helicopters

A storm survivor is airlifted to safety

Sunlight streams through the damaged roof of the Superdome

Storm survivors receive food from the National Guard

GULF COAST

FEMA trailers appear all over the Gulf Coast to house the homeless

President George W. Bush at a conference on Katrina

A volunteer rebuilds a home destroyed by Katrina

Gulf Coast residents pose outside their new home

Some decisions made during the emergency were mistakes. It was likely a bad decision to bus people to the Superdome rather than out of the city. Was there time to bus to safer, better-equipped places? Could people needing medical help have received better care elsewhere?

People don't agree on the answers to these questions. But according to an interview with Paul Harris, one of the refugees at the Superdome, "We kept hearing stories that the buses were coming, the buses were coming. Of course they didn't come. And that's what led to the lack of trust that made it seem like anything might be true."

Kim Murphy, a reporter for the *Los Angeles Times*, wrote, "Everybody who was nobody in New Orleans was there . . . people with no prayer of getting out of town and no shelter but the massive stadium that became, for six awful days, a sweltering cesspool of human misery."

With the power out, it was nearly impossible to coordinate efforts between rescue groups. No backup communications plan was in place. The almost complete lack of communication led to false reports in the media about what was going on in New Orleans. Untrue stories of widespread looting, gunfire, and violence caused people to panic. The reports also made rescue teams and others afraid to come into the city to help.

Local agencies blamed FEMA for not helping enough. FEMA blamed local agencies for not asking for help soon enough. When President Bush finally visited the ravaged city on Friday, September 2, he told Michael Brown, the director of FEMA, "Brownie, you're doing a heck of a job." Ten days later, Brown resigned after what many called a botched response to the hurricane's destruction.

Michael Brown

Some engineers believe that the failure of many levees could have been prevented. For years, there was talk of installing floodgates. In a superstorm, the floodgates would close to prevent storm surges from raising the water level in the canals. But disagreements in local government prevented the building of floodgates. Instead, the levees along the canals were topped with concrete flood walls that didn't offer enough protection.

The Army Corps of Engineers was blamed for the levee failures. It happened because of the bad design and construction of the levees. The Army engineers may have been responsible for the weak levee designs and construction, but a law that was written in 1928 protected them. The court battles were still going on in 2014.

The hurricane hit New Orleans's poorest people the hardest. Often, surviving family members were separated from each other. People moved away. Some never returned. The National

Lieutenant General
Carl Strock of the
Army Corps

Guard and other law-enforcement agencies were called in to keep order. Many people attempted to move back to their city but were forced to leave by police and soldiers. They were not allowed back into their own homes until power was restored. People became frustrated and angry. Hurricane Katrina and the failure of the New Orleans levees didn't just destroy homes and businesses and take lives. The effects of Hurricane Katrina caused people to lose trust in their own government.

Stuck in the Superdome

An evacuation plan for the Superdome called for hundreds of buses. Buses became available, but finding drivers was difficult. Drivers were often afraid of entering the city because of the reports about violence. Finally on Saturday, September 3, 2005, the last refugees in the Superdome were rescued. They climbed on buses and headed for other shelters in other states. Many were sent to Houston's NRG Astrodome. It would not be home. But at least it would be better than the Superdome. As Louis Dalmas Sr. said, "I feel like I've been here forty years. Any bus going anywhere—that's all I want." He was one of the last people to get out of the Superdome after Hurricane Katrina.

CHAPTER 8
A Slow Recovery

Hurricane Katrina damaged about ninety thousand square miles of the Gulf Coast. That's an area almost as big as the state of Oregon. Almost as soon as the storm stopped, recovery began.

Work began immediately to fix the levees, canals, and pumping stations in New Orleans.

Thousands of sandbags were used as temporary fixes. It took more than a year to repair the major breaches. Even after that, the levees still needed rebuilding.

Canals were repaired and power was restored so that pumps could pump out the floodwater. Portable pumps were brought in, as well. At one point, over 100,000 gallons of water were being pumped out of New Orleans every second. That amounted to about 120,000 full bathtubs a minute! Eventually, the patchwork of walls and levees was replaced. Billions of dollars were spent on over a hundred miles of new levees, flood walls, storm-proof pumps, and gates.

Congress changed the way emergencies are managed and reorganized FEMA. Funding was also provided to upgrade communication networks and build new ones. The National Emergency Communications Plan was created to improve communications systems in any

emergency, especially in high-risk areas. Upgrades and changes also helped make it easier for different agencies to work together.

Over a million people from the Gulf Coast had left their homes. These refugees were scattered all over the United States. Some moved in with friends or relatives. Others stayed in hotels and even on the cruise ships that had become shelters.

About twenty-five thousand people were bused to the Houston Astrodome in Texas, nearly 350 miles away. Some people were stuck in temporary shelters for days, weeks, or even months.

New Orleans, the city whose motto was "Let the good times roll," had been flattened. As people were slowly allowed back into their neighborhoods, they faced the huge job of rebuilding their homes and their lives. Very few needed shelter for only a short time and then returned home. People lived for months in their upper stories while the flooded lower levels were repaired. Blue tarps were seen all over the city. The tarps kept rain out of houses with damaged roofs. But thousands of other homes were beyond repair. In all, over two hundred thousand homes were damaged or destroyed.

When a neighborhood is destroyed, cleanup and recovery often become a group effort. People from all over the United States wanted to help the victims of Hurricane Katrina. They sent money, clothing, and other supplies. Church groups and many other community organizations donated their time and energy to help. Relief agencies, such as the Salvation Army and the American Red Cross, set up stations to provide food and other supplies.

A school in St. Bernard Parish opened in less than three months. A collection of tents and trailers was put together. Generators provided electricity. The principal, Wayne Warner, said, "It was the first time we saw people smile . . . They realized things were going to be kind of normal. It wasn't going to be the same, but it was going to be all right."

The need for housing was greater than anyone was prepared for. The large-scale housing challenge was like nothing before in the history of the United States, and it proved to be too much for FEMA.

In one effort to provide temporary housing, the agency ordered about two hundred thousand trailers and mobile homes. But FEMA didn't realize that only a few thousand units could be built in a month. And when they were finished, many of the trailers had problems. For example, locks were a security risk, because the same key

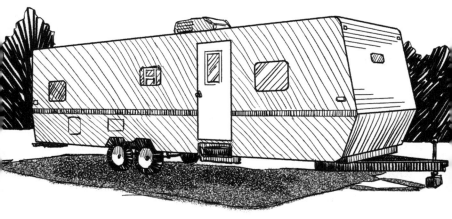

could open a lot of trailer doors. Even worse, some trailers were delivered with high levels of toxic gas called *formaldehyde*. Anybody who lived in them became very sick.

It was often weeks or months before electricity or drinkable water were available. Part of the Lower Ninth Ward had a "boil water" order in place the longest. A "boil water" order meant that water wasn't safe to drink unless it was boiled first. The order was finally removed over a year after Hurricane Katrina hit New Orleans.

It seemed that nothing was easy anymore in the Big Easy. Jim Pate remembers what it was like. "In those first deep, dark months after Katrina, everything you saw around you was gray," he said. "Even all the birds had left." Pate was the executive director of Habitat for Humanity in the New Orleans area. Habitat for Humanity helps people own their own homes, often by building new ones for them. Their volunteers responded

to the Katrina disaster throughout the gulf states. In a few years, they had repaired or built more than 2,200 houses in the hardest-hit areas of the gulf. At least for some, things were looking up.

But it took a very long time before much of New Orleans showed real signs of recovery. Over 70,000 people still lived in FEMA trailers in 2006. It wasn't until 2012 that nobody was living in one. Mitchell Landrieu became mayor in 2010. He funded more construction projects for the damaged neighborhoods. By August 2013, over 130,000 homeowners had received grants

and loans to help rebuild their homes. Even so, a lot of abandoned space remained in the city.

By 2012, the population of New Orleans was about 370,000. That is 76 percent of its pre-Katrina population. It means that one out of every four people living in New Orleans before the storm never came back. There are about 100,000 fewer African Americans living there. Even so, African Americans still make up the majority of the city's population.

However, people continue to return to New Orleans, and new people are moving in, too. In 2012, according to the US Census Bureau, New Orleans was the fastest-growing city in the United States.

Ronald Lewis was one of the thousands whose community in the Lower Ninth Ward was washed away. In 2013, some flood-damaged homes in his neighborhood were still boarded up. But there were new houses, too. Many of them were built on stilts, in order to avoid flooding in the future.

Ronald has a shed in his backyard that is filled with memories of the disaster. The collection includes the MREs and scrapbooks that show the way people had to live after losing everything. Ronald says the collection reminds him that, "We had lost everything, but we didn't lose hope. So every piece in here is symbolic of that—of people wanting to share in the story of us rising up out of the ruins of Katrina and saying, 'We're here, we're back.'"

CHAPTER 9
Climate Change

People in the gulf and other coastal regions are used to hurricanes. In spite of the risks, they continue to move to the coast or go there for vacation. Tourism, oil and natural gas, shipping ports, and fishing are all huge coastal industries. Should people living in coastal areas be worried about climate change? Yes.

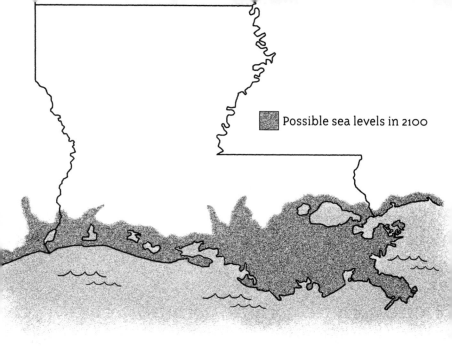

Possible sea levels in 2100

In the spring of 2014, the National Climate Assessment was published. The report took four years to prepare and involved more than three hundred scientists. It showed that since 1895, the average air temperature has increased by 1.5°F. Most of that rise has been since 1980. According to the Environmental Protection Agency, temperatures are expected to rise by up to 10°F by the end of the twenty-first century.

The surface temperature of oceans is also getting warmer, causing sea levels to rise. That is because the warmer ocean water swells in a process called *thermal expansion*. The warmer water also melts ice in the polar regions and throughout the world's glaciers. At the rate global warming

is going, by the year 2100, sea levels could be five to six feet higher than they were in 2014!

Scientists know that there have always been sea-level changes due to natural causes. But current studies point to greenhouse gases as the main driving force behind warmer air, warmer ocean temperatures, and rising sea levels. Greenhouse gases are produced mostly by gas emissions from burning fossil fuels for electricity, heat, and transportation. Greenhouse gases trap heat, causing the earth to get warmer.

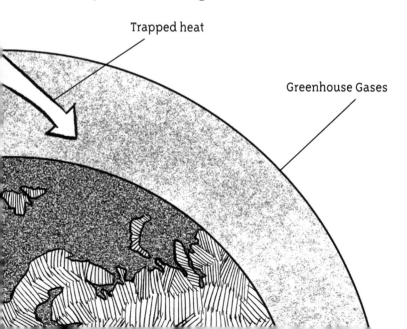

Trapped heat

Greenhouse Gases

How does climate change make it riskier to live in places like New Orleans? Islands near a coast are called *barrier islands*. These islands are eroding away as the sea level rises. Barrier islands help to absorb the force of hurricanes. They can even slow down storm surges, kind of like speed bumps. Millions of dollars have been spent to try to rebuild barrier islands in the Gulf Coast region. But they are not as strong as the original islands, which formed over time from sand and added sediment from the Mississippi River.

Rising sea levels and warmer ocean temperatures mean more powerful storms. In fact, most scientists agree that global warming is already having an effect on the number and power of hurricanes. In the Atlantic and Pacific, storms increased in intensity by about 50 percent compared to storms before 1970. Warmer water and fewer barrier islands are allowing hurricanes to become larger, last longer, and cause more destruction.

The amount of precipitation (rainfall) has also gone up. The increase could be too much for the new levee system around New Orleans. The system was built to prevent the kind of flooding that occurred from Hurricane Katrina. But it appears that future storms and flooding could be even worse than what Katrina brought with it.

What can be done? Nature will always challenge us, but human-caused problems can be resolved if people cooperate. In 2015, US President Barack Obama enacted the Clean Power Plan to help cut down greenhouse gases that fuel global warming.

The plan did things such as limit carbon pollution from power plants, promote the use of renewable energy, and work to cut energy waste in homes and businesses.

The US Environmental Protection Agency  had already started to regulate greenhouse gases under the Clean Air Act in early 2011. But in 2017, President Donald J. Trump rolled back these regulations.

Was Hurricane Katrina a wake-up call? A lot of people hope so. But that remains to be seen.

A Record-Breaking Year

In 2020, there were 30 named storms, more than any time in history. It was only the second time that Greek letters had to be used. (The first time had been in 2005.)

Arthur	Kyle	Wilfred
Bertha	Laura	Alpha
Cristobal	Marco	Beta
Dolly	Nana	Gamma
Edouard	Omar	Delta
Fay	Paulette	Epsilon
Gonzalo	Rene	Zeta
Hanna	Sally	Eta
Isaias	Teddy	Theta
Josephine	Vicky	Iota

Timeline of Hurricane Katrina

- The first weather advisory about the hurricane that would become Katrina is issued by the National Hurricane Center.
- 11 a.m.: The storm is named Katrina. It is the eleventh named storm of 2005.
- Katrina is now a Category 1 hurricane. It makes its first landfall on Florida's southeastern coast.
- Hurricane Katrina is getting stronger by the hour. It has winds of about a hundred miles an hour. The governors of Mississippi and Louisiana declare states of emergency.
- Evacuation begins in three states. Katrina is close to becoming a Category 4 hurricane.
- The mayor of New Orleans issues a mandatory evacuation order. People are bused to the Superdome and other "shelters of last resort." Katrina is now a Category 5 hurricane.
- Hurricane Katrina makes landfall in Louisiana with winds of up to 145 miles an hour. The levees in New Orleans are breaching or collapsing. Water is pouring into the city and rising fast. Katrina later hits Biloxi and Gulfport, Mississippi, destroying most of both cities.
- The National Hurricane Center reports that the storm has winds of about thirty-five miles an hour, and there is heavy rainfall. It is the last advisory on Hurricane Katrina. The mayor of New Orleans orders a complete mandatory evacuation as the city continues to flood.

Friday, September 2, 2005	President George W. Bush, signs a $10.5 billion relief package.
Saturday, September 3, 2005	The last refugees in the Superdome are rescued.
Tuesday, September 6, 2005	The mayor of New Orleans orders that people be removed by force from the city.
Monday, September 19, 2005	People who had been allowed back into New Orleans are evacuated again because of Hurricane Rita.
Saturday, September 24, 2005	Hurricane Rita makes landfall just west of where Katrina hit.
Tuesday, October 4, 2005	The official death toll from Hurricane Katrina is estimated at over 1,800. Most of the deaths were in Louisiana. Hundreds of people are still missing.
Thursday, April 6, 2006	The name Katrina is retired from the list of hurricane names. It is designated the most destructive storm in US history.

Bibliography

*Books for young readers

Brinkley, Douglas. *The Great Deluge: Hurricane Katrina, New Orleans, and the Mississippi Gulf Coast*. New York: William Morrow, 2006.

*Fradin, Judith Bloom and Dennis Brindell Fradin. *Hurricane Katrina.* Tarrytown, NY: Cavendish, 2009.

*Hoena, Blake. *Hurricane Katrina: An Interactive Modern History Adventure.* Minneapolis: Capstone Press, 2014.

**Hurricane Katrina: A chronology*. Reuters. Slideshow. http://www.reuters.com/news/pictures/slideshow?articleId=USRTR246V7#a=1

*Larson, Kirby. *Two Bobbies: A True Story of Hurricane Katrina, Friendship, and Survival.* New York: Macmillan, 2008.

Neff, Thomas. *Holding Out and Hanging On: Surviving Hurricane Katrina.* Columbia University of Missouri Press, 2007.

*Pietras, Jamie. *Hurricane Katrina*. New York: Chelsea House Publishers, 2008.

*Uhlberg, Myron. *A Storm Called Katrina*. Atlanta: Peachtree Publishers, 2011.

van Heerden, Ivor and Mike Bryan. *The Storm: What Went Wrong and Why During Hurricane Katrina—the Inside Story from One Louisiana Scientist*. New York: Viking, 2006.